INDEX

ISIS: The bloody Caliphate

Erdogan: The Sultan's Empire

Jeb BUSH 2016: The Clan is back

Hillary for President? Not in my Name

Far Left Terrorism

Because unemployment is so pervasive, jobless, disenchanted people are joining radical parties espousing a wide variety of ideologies. Examples include populist euro-skeptic parties, such as Italy's Five Star movement; far-right parties, such as Greece's Golden Dawn party; and anti-austerity leftist groups, such as Greece's Coalition of the Radical Left, or Syriza. With unemployment in Greece at 27 percent, it is not surprising to see both radical right-wing and radical left-wing groups gaining support from those who have become deeply disaffected by the crises.

In fact, Greece has a long history of left-wing radicalism inclined toward violence. The 1970s saw the rise of radical group *17 November*, and more recent years marked the rise of such groups as the *Revolutionary Struggle* and the *Conspiracy of Fire Cells*.

Given this history and the manner in which the current crises are producing disaffected, radicalized and unemployed people, we thought it would be worth examining radical far-left groups in Greece and the types of violence they can be expected to conduct.

It is also important to remember that Greece is not the only country in which the population, particularly the left, is radicalizing. Italy, too, has seen increased leftist radicalism. What is happening in these two countries could herald things to come elsewhere in Europe.

A History of Radicalism

The revolutionary left in Greece dates back to the anarchists of the 1800s and the emergence of communism in Europe. Influenced by the Bolshevik Revolution in Russia, communist partisans were some of the most effective anti-Nazi forces during the Axis powers' brutal occupation of Greece (Italy and Bulgaria joined Germany in the occupation). After the Allied invasion of Greece and its liberation from Axis control, a civil war erupted that pitted communist partisans against anti-communist forces, which were backed by the British and the Americans. Because many former Nazi collaborators aided the anti-communists in the Greek Civil War, many anti-communist elements remained in Greece's security forces. The war also left the remnants of an embittered communist movement upset by the fact that Nazi collaborators such as Georgios Papadopoulos, who would become the future leader of a military junta that seized power in 1967, were never brought to justice.

Like much of Europe, Greece then became a Cold War battleground. The strength of the communist forces in Greece and in its neighbor, Turkey, was the driving force behind the 1947 Truman Doctrine in which U.S. President Harry S. Truman pledged military and economic support to Greece and Turkey to prevent them from falling into the Soviet sphere of influence. This resulted in strong anti-U.S. and anti-NATO sentiment among the Greek left, which would later act on that sentiment through terrorist activity.

But the United States and its allies were not the only ones attempting to influence Greece. The Soviet Union saw the Greek communists, like communist groups elsewhere in the West, as a useful tool. The Soviets actively supported communist activists in the Greek labor and student movements. Anti-regime radicalism in the Greek student movement came to a head in 1973, when student protests against the military junta were put down by force. In a particularly iconic incident, an army tank crashed through the gates of Athens Polytechnic on Nov. 17, 1973, as soldiers seized control of the university from student protesters.

The gravity of the Athens Polytechnic uprising was clearly felt when a then-unknown group, *Revolutionary Organization 17 November*, assassinated Richard Welch, the CIA station chief in Athens, in December 1975.

From then until 2000, 17 November conducted several assassinations and attacked NATO, Greek government and Greek industrialist targets. Although the group came to be known for close-quarter assassinations using .45-caliber pistols, they also conducted a number of successful bombing attacks, such as the June 1988 assassination of U.S. Defense Attache Capt. William Nordeen. In 1989, the group stole anti-tank rockets from a military base in Larissa. The rockets were later used in attacks against buildings and armored limousines.

The 17 November operatives practiced good terrorist tradecraft and excellent operational security. This allowed them to operate far longer than their contemporary radical leftist groups in Germany and Italy. While the founders of the German Red Army Faction and the Italian Red Brigades were arrested in the 1970s, the founders of 17 November were not taken into custody until 2002, when a botched bombing on a ferry company resulted in the arrest of the bomber. Authorities used the evidence the culprit provided to arrest most of the remaining members of 17 November, whose long reign of terror finally came to an end.

Links with SYRIZA

The publication of an autobiographical book written by one of November 17's leaders, **Dimitris Koufontinas**, has triggered a new clash between New Democracy and SYRIZA.

The coalition government party issued a statement explaining that the introduction to the book was written by **Nikos Giannopoulos**, a founding member of "Roza" (a political group that was later integrated in SYRIZA party) and insinuated that SYRIZA offered support to terrorism.

Mr. Giannopoulos also explained that he was never a member of the opposition party and that he testified as a defense witness at the 17N trials as a founding a member of the Network for Political and Social Rights, arguing that 17N was being persecuted for political purposes.

But Greece was not quiet for long. Inspired by the highly publicized arrest and trial of the 17 November members, a new group arose from the radical Greek left in 2003. This group was called Revolutionary Struggle. The group shared 17 November's anti-imperialist, anti-capitalist and anti-U.S. focus, but it was more anarchistic than the Marxist 17 November.

From 2003 to 2010, Revolutionary Struggle bombed several Greek law enforcement buildings, banks and international corporations. The group was also responsible for a number of firearm attacks against police and a rocket attack against the U.S. Embassy. In the latter attack, the group notably used an RPG-7, not the M28 super bazooka rockets associated with 17 November. The rocket-propelled grenade launcher was recovered in April 2010, when six members of Revolutionary Struggle were arrested. Two members of the group, founder Nikos Maziotis and his wife, Panagiota Roupa, fled after being released from custody during their trial in July 2012.

In 2008, another Greek anarchist group calling itself the *Conspiracy of Fire Cells* announced its presence with a series of low-level bombing attacks against car dealerships and banks in Athens and Thessaloniki. Until late 2010, the group's attacks were meant to damage property and send messages rather than kill people — a big departure from the homicidal intentions of 17 November. In the January 2010 bombing of the Greek Parliament, the group made a warning call to a newspaper that permitted the area to be evacuated, thus avoiding casualties.

This operational paradigm changed dramatically in 2010, when the group began to send letter bombs. After a number of letter bombs were sent to the Greek Ministry of Justice, foreign embassies in Athens and German

Chancellor Angela Merkel, Greek police arrested two suspects. At the time of the arrests, the suspects were found to be in possession of letter bombs addressed to then-French President Nicolas Sarkozy's office in Paris and to the Belgian and Dutch embassies in Athens. In total, 13 people were arrested and charged for their involvement in the Conspiracy of Fire Cells letter bomb campaign.

In the weeks before their trial in January 2011, anarchists in Italy mailed letter bombs packed with shrapnel to several embassies in Rome. On Dec. 28, 2010, anarchists attacked the Greek Embassy in Buenos Aires, which was followed by a bombing attack on the Athens courthouse in which the Conspiracy of Fire Cells members were to be tried. The courthouse bombing involved a substantial device that damaged the building and several nearby vehicles, but because of a warning call placed to authorities 40 minutes before the device detonated, it inflicted no casualties.

A group calling itself the Lambros Fountas cell of the Informal Anarchist Federation claimed responsibility for the Rome parcel bombs. (*Lambros Fountas was a member of Revolutionary Struggle who was killed in April 2010 and whose death led to the roundup of the group's members.*) The moniker shows the close relationship between Greek and Italian anarchists. Attacks in Italy, such as the May 2012 shooting of a nuclear engineer in Genoa, and two attempts to sabotage rail signaling cables in Bristol, the United Kingdom, have been claimed by people operating under the name of the Informal Anarchist Federation.

In one of the most brazen attacks in recent years, three armed men appeared at Microsoft's Athens office in the early hours of June 27, 2012, and, after forcing out the security guards, they backed a van up to the doors of the building and ignited a large incendiary device, which damaged the building.

More recently, anarchists in Greece have conducted small-scale arson and bombing attacks against bank branches, political parties and the homes of journalists. On March 11, 2013, they conducted a low-level bombing attack against a courier company in Athens.

Progressing Toward Lethality

From this history, we can identify some trends for future radical activity. First, it's clear that the Marxist terrorism that wracked Europe in the 1970s and 1980s is not about to return, no matter how many people are radicalized by the current crises. The geopolitical environment that spawned and nurtured Marxist terrorism has changed dramatically. The state-sponsored training and support that many European Marxist groups received from the Soviet Union and Eastern European states, such as East Germany, simply will not reappear. In addition, the Marxist training camps European militants were able to visit in such places as Yemen, Libya and Iraq no longer exist.

Since the fall of the Soviet Union, most left-wing radicals, save for some in Latin America, have become disillusioned with Marxism. This has helped foster the growth of anarchism, which is seen by many radicals as a system that is less prone to corruption and is therefore a more viable alternative to the capitalist imperialist system.

Something that has remained consistent among those in the radical left is the sense of international solidarity. It was this solidarity that drew Japanese Red Army operatives to conduct attacks in the name of their Palestinian comrades and inspired the Provisional Irish Republican Army to train other Marxist revolutionaries in bomb making tradecraft in training camps in southern Yemen. Likewise, present-day Italian and Argentine anarchists claim attacks for their imprisoned Greek comrades.

While Greek and other European anarchists have shared the Marxists' anti-capitalist and anti-imperialist beliefs, they have yet to kill people to the extent the Marxists did in their attacks. Bombing an ATM or setting a building on fire is a far cry from kidnapping or assassinating a banker or industrialist. Sending a letter bomb to an embassy is also quite different from the Nordeen and Welch assassinations.

Nevertheless, the shift from attacks meant to cause property destruction to attacks meant to maim people — sending letter bombs or kneecapping a nuclear engineer, for example — is quite disturbing. If the trend continues, it will not be a far jump to conduct attacks meant to cause fatalities. The Revolutionary Struggle already made this jump in their attacks against Greek police targets, and other anarchists could follow suit. The fact that Italian anarchists have included shrapnel in their letter bombs is another disturbing indicator that they may be making a similar progression toward lethality.

The January 11, 2013, firebombing attacks against the homes of five journalists in Greece is also unsettling in that it brought violence to the homes, rather than the business offices, of the targets. Fire can be a very deadly weapon, and if the firebombing attacks against homes continue, it is only a matter of time before someone dies.

Although today's anarchists lack the state sponsorship the Cold War-era European Marxist groups enjoyed in terms of funding and obtaining weapons, the proximity of places like Greece and Italy to the black arms markets in the Balkans and the Middle East means that they will be able to readily obtain arms. The rocket-propelled grenade launcher and the Serbian Zastava pistols found in the possession of Revolutionary Struggle militants at the time of their arrests is a great example of the availability of arms in the region.

Whereas Molotov cocktails, camping gas canister bombs and letter bombs are fairly cheap, guns and rocket launchers cost real money on the black market. Therefore, it will be important to see if Greek anarchists begin moneymaking operations, such as bank robberies and high-value kidnappings for ransom. Since anarchists tend to be more plugged in to technology, indications of cybercrime should also be looked for.

Because the anarchist movement is so interconnected, shifts in violence in places like Greece and Italy can quickly translate into continent-wide, even global, trends.

17N and Syriza connections

The characteristic pathologies of two dysfunctional states allow "Revolutionary Organization 17 November" to keep damaging U.S.-Greek relations 13 years after 17N's collapse in July 2002. Ambassador Pearce's press statement regarding therelease of convicted 17N member Savvas Xiros ("a profoundly unfriendly act") is the most vigorous public U.S. Embassy intervention in Greek politics since the Athens Olympics in 2004. So how concerned should Greeks be about the future of Greek-U.S. relations if Xiros indeed goes home wearing an ankle bracelet?

This is an unnecessary crisis, of course. The humanitarian issue of Xiros's medical condition could have been handled within the existing legal framework were the Greek justice system not in a state of semi-collapse. Even the Colonels accepted the principle of Greek juriprudence (though not U.S), that prisoners, including bomb-planting revolutionaries, should be released if their imprisonment causes "incurable harm" to their health. This is a provision that has been abused, for example to release Grigoris Michalopoulos, the notorious publisher/extortionist who had a note from his cardiologist.
But Xiros's disabilities, not all of them the result of the bomb that blew up in his hands, are real

Since judicial officials shrink from such difficult decisions, the Tsipras government drafted a law that takes responsibility for Xiros's release away from them. By so doing, Syriza hoped to reassure its internal opposition that it still loved the Revolution no matter how ardently Finance Minister Varoufakis might flirt with Christine Lagarde. But the gesture triggered an instinctive overreaction from a superpower still deeply irrational 14 years after 9/11.

The excuse offered by State Department spokesperson Harf for the blistering American reaction, that Xiros "would be in position to resume terrorist plotting and planning," is fairly stupid. More than half the known members of 17N are out of jail already, and all of them are now docile good citizens. Xiros's current obsessions, at least his public ones, are not revolutionary. Sending home a mostly blind, somewhat deaf, partly mangled, and mystically addled icon painter will not encourage more terrorist attacks on U.S. interests.

One reason for overreaction is that the Embassy's diplomatic staff has turned over three times since 17N was arrested. The current incumbents may be unaware that 17N was convicted on the basis of confessions signed by Savvas Xiros and his brothers. Those confessions are not complete or truthful -- we do not really know who pulled the trigger in 17N's 23 murders -- but we do know they were extracted through an unofficial promise of more lenient treatment than 17N's crimes deserved. The cruelest way to neutralize Xiros as a revolutionary would be to respect that promise and thereby underscore the importance of his role in informing on his comrades.

A key task of the Greek or any state that sincerely wishes to eliminate terrorism is to demonstrate that its justice is superior to that offered by its foes. The failure of the Greek state to punish Junta torturers adequately opened a political window for 17N in 1975. Allowing Xiros's family to assume responsibility for his medical care would be a small but useful gesture, one that stands in pointed contrast to the callous indifference with which 17N selected and murdered its victims. We should not underestimate the impact of such magnanimity on young men who have been indoctrinated to treat the state simultaneously as predator and prey.

Americans are not interested in the effectiveness argument. They are encouraged to believe, against masses of countervailing evidence (including an anti-U.S. bomber named Kostas Simitis), that there is a specific category of human beings called terrorists who, like the zombies in video games, must be ruthlessly exterminated. And the families of the American victims are naturally grateful to be told their legitimate grief and anger are a patriotic sentiment. For bureaucrats and politicians to thrive, such anger must be seen to have consequences.

In the short-term, U.S. anger at the home confinement of Savvas Xiros will translate into an increase in the political cost to the Obama administration of continuing to treat Greece as a valued ally. The U.S. counterterrorism community can afford to be spiteful, since Greece -- with a negligible terrorism profile these days -- is an expendable partner. If a clash occurs over Ukraine sanctions and Russia's economic leverage, the bureaucratic coalition against Greece will become dangerously powerful. One early casualty could be Greece's continued participation in the visa waiver program, a painful measure for the U.S. Embassy but one justifiable by Greek migration statistics.

The important point to remember is that the United States cares far more about the health of the European Union and the global financial system than it does about Greece. If the Tsipras government continues to seem aggressively ambivalent about its desire for rescue within that system, the U.S. government will watch from the sidelines as it sinks. In this larger context, the release or not of Savvas Xiros should be seen by all sides as a trivial footnote.

Alexis Tsipras

Alexis Tsipras was born in 1974 in Athens. He received his civil engineering degree from the National Technical University of Athens, where he also completed postgraduate studies in Urban and Regional Planning. He worked as a civil engineer in the construction industry and conducted a series of studies regarding urban planning in Athens.

He joined the Left while still in high school and actively participated in the pupils' movement during '90-'91; he continued his commitment at university in the student movement.

In 1999 he was elected Secretary of the Youth of Synaspismos, a position he maintained until March 2003. During the 4th Congress of Synaspismos (December 2004) he was elected to the Central Political Committee and also to the Political Secretariat of the Party, where he was responsible for Education and Youth policies.

In October 2006 he was a Mayoral candidate for the city of Athens, representing the municipal movement "Open City", which came in third with a percentage of 10,5%. During the 5th Congress of Synaspismos (February 2008), he was elected President of the Party.

In the national elections of 2009 he was elected Member of the Greek Parliament and became Chairman of the parliamentary group of SYRIZA. During the 3rd Congress of the European Left Party (December 2010) in Paris, he was elected Vice President.

Since the general election of 2012 when he was re-elected as a Member of Parliament, he is Leader of the Main Opposition in Greece. During the 4th Congress of the European Left Party (December 2013), he was nominated as a candidate for the Presidency of the European Commission and was also re-elected Vice President of the European Left Party.

SYRIZA and Chavez

Greece's new Syriza is not only demanding a haircut from the rest of the European Union of nearly $200 billion, or 88% of the Greek GDP. It is also pushing for a fundamental change in Europe's foreign policy, from a pro-Atlantic orientation to a pro-Russian one.

Syriza is not a friend of Israel or NATO, either. Spain seems to be following suit. Neither Syriza nor Podemos is expected to install a Stalinist dictatorship, but two things are beyond doubt. The Marxist economic remedies that these parties stand for will not lead to more prosperity for their countries, nor will the transatlantic relations between Europe and the United States much improve.

One aspect of the Greek elections to which not much attention has been paid are the consequences for NATO. The huge victory of the extreme-left Syriza party marks the first time that the Far Left takes over a NATO country. In a sense, it is a vindication for the Communists, who lost the Greek civil war in 1949.

Syriza leader Alexis Tsipras, the new Greek Prime Minister, began his political career as an activist of the youth section of the Communist Party. Later, he became the leader of Synaspismos and its successor party Syriza. Both were a coalition of Marxist parties including the Communists and Maoists. The 40-year old Tsipras is an admirer of revolutionary leaders such as Fidel Castro, Ernesto Che Guevara and Hugo Chavez. He named his son Ernesto after the Argentinean-Cuban revolutionary. Two years ago, he flew to Caracas, Venezuela, to attend the funeral of Chavez.

Many of the new Greek ministers are former members of the Communist Party of Greece [KKE]. Nikos Kotzias, the new minister of Foreign Affairs, was a member of the Central Committee of the KKE. Other prominent Communists in the new Greek cabinet are Giorgios Stathakis, the Minister of Economics and Infrastructure, Panaghiotis Lafazanis, the Minister of Energy, and Panos Skourletis, the Minister of Labor and Social Solidarity. Yiannis Dragasakis, also a former member of the Central Committee of the KKE, is Greece's new Deputy Prime Minister. Although the new finance minister, Yanis Varoufakis, does not have a past in the KKE, he is an economist who describes himself as a libertarian Marxist.

The new Greek cabinet is not a friend of Israel nor of Jews. Syriza is known for its anti-Israeli and pro-Palestinian positions. Syriza politicians have frequently participated in protests against the Jewish state. Clause 38 of the Syriza party program advocates the "abolition of military cooperation with Israel" and "support for the creation of a Palestinian state within the 1967 borders."

Syriza is not a friend of NATO, either. Clause 40 of the party program advocates the "closure of all foreign bases in Greece and withdrawal from NATO." Although no one expects the Syriza government actually to live up to its promise to withdraw Greece from NATO, the change of course in Greece's foreign policy became apparent on its first day in office, when the new cabinet distanced itself from an EU statement protesting Russian actions in Ukraine and threatening further sanctions against Moscow.

Foreign Minister Nikos Kotzias has been a lifelong ally of whoever is a hardliner in Moscow. In the 1980s, he praised the Communist crackdown on the Solidarity movement in Poland. Today, he is close to the Russian political philosopher Alexander Dugin, an ideologue of the anti-democratic and fiercely anti-American National Bolshevist movement and leader of the Eurasia Party, who wants to restore the Russian Empire as the leading nation of a territorial bloc encompassing the Eurasian landmass. In April 2013, Kotzias invited Dugin to give a lecture at the University of Piraeus, Greece.

Syriza is not only demanding a debt haircut from the rest of European Union of €173.2 billion ($196bn), or 88% of the Greek GDP, making it the biggest debt reduction in history. It is also pushing for a fundamental change in the EU's foreign policy, from a pro-Atlantic orientation towards a pro-Russian one.

Meanwhile, the electoral success of Syriza is inspiring others. Last Sunday, up to 100,000 Spaniards attended a rally in the Spanish capital Madrid. The rally was organized by Podemos, a party established less than one year ago which, according to polls, could become the largest party in this year's general elections. Like Syriza's Alexis Tsipras, Podemos' leader, the 36-year old Pablo Iglesias, is a former member of the Communist Party and an admirer of the late Venezuelan dictator Hugo Chavez. The three main leaders of Podemos even sat on the board of a foundation that, over the course of the past decade, received at least €3.7m ($4 million) from the Venezuelan government for so-called political advisory work.

Hence, the prospect of a far-left party winning the Spanish elections later this year, thus vindicating the Communists who lost the Spanish civil war, is a real possibility.

Of course, history never repeats itself. Neither Syriza nor Podemos is expected to install a Stalinist dictatorship, but two things are beyond doubt. The Marxist economic remedies that these parties stand for will not lead to more prosperity for their countries, nor will the transatlantic relations between Europe and the United States much improve with governments whose leaders draw their inspiration from Hugo Chavez.

SYRIZA and Putin

After a landslide victory in the early parliamentary elections held on 25 January 2015, the Greek Coalition of the Radical Left (SYRIZA) that secured 149 seats in the new parliament has surprised the left-wing voters and sympathizers by agreeing to form, already on 26 January, a coalition government with the far right Independent Greeks party (ANEL) that now has 13 seats. Popular support for the neo-Nazi Golden Dawn led by currently imprisoned Nikolaos Michaloliakos has slightly decreased: the neo-Nazis have secured 17 seats (one seat less than in 2012), but the Golden Dawn is still the third largest party in Greece.

Both SYRIZA and ANEL are so-called "anti-austerity parties" implying that they oppose reducing budget deficits as a response to the Greek financial crisis, as well as rejecting the austerity package put forth by the EU and the IMF. The "anti-austerity" platform may seem the only agenda that has drawn the two parties they share, but they also share a similar approach to foreign policy issues - an approach that may undermine the EU unity over the Russian threat.

Both parties are overtly pro-Russian, and SYRIZA's leader Alexis Tsipras denounced the sanctions against Russia imposed by the EU for Russia's annexation of Crimea and its invasion of Ukraine that has already cost Ukrainians thousands of lives.

In May 2014, i.e. already after Russia had started its invasion of Ukraine, Tsipras travelled to Moscow to meet Vladimir Putin's major allies such as Valentina Matviyenko, chairman of Federation Council of the Russian Federation, and Aleksey Pushkov, chairman of the Russian parliament's foreign affairs committee. Both Matviyenko and Pushkov are sanctioned by the US, while Matviyenko is also sanctioned by the EU. This did not prevent Tsipras from holding a meeting with her.

According to Aleksandr Dugin, the "father" of Eurasia political theory,: "*In Greece, our* [i.e. Russia's] *partners could eventually be Leftists from SYRIZA, which refuses Atlanticism, liberalism and the domination of the forces of global finance. As far as I know, SYRIZA is anti-capitalist and it is critical of the global oligarchy that has victimized Greece and Cyprus. The case of SYRIZA is interesting because of its far-Left attitude toward the liberal global system. It is a good sign that such non-conformist forces have appeared on the scene.*"

The pro-Russian sentiments of SYRIZA were manifested, in particular, in its voting behavior in the European parliament. For example, on 16 September 2014, when the European Parliament ratified the EU-Ukraine Association agreement - an agreement that was one of the reasons of the Russian invasion of Ukraine - all six MEPs of SYRIZA voted against the ratification of this agreement.

If SYRIZA is Russia's "Trojan horse" in the EU, then ANEL led by Panos Kammenos may be even worse.

ANEL (founded in February 2012) is a far right party described as "highly conservative and nationalistic right-wing". In its opposition to immigration and multiculturalism, ANEL is similar to, yet is more moderate than, the neo-Nazi Golden Dawn. ANEL is also prone to conspiracy theories. Anti-Semitism is not alien to ANEL either: "Panos Kammenos, speaking on a TV program made the baseless claim that Jewish people in Greece are not taxed in contrast to Christian Orthodox Greeks".

The driving force behind the pro-Russian approach of ANEL seems to be Gavriil Avramidis, who was elected MP with ANEL in Thessaloniki in 2012. He is also head of the Patriotic Social Movement "Greek-Russian Alliance" founded in 2001 and aimed at widening co-operation between Greece and Russia.

Yet Avramidis may be not the only politician in ANEL who is lobbying Russian interests in Greece. Kammenos visited Moscow in the first half of January 2015. Moreover, an article titled "An Attempt at Reviving the Russian Party" that was published on 22 January in the Greek Russian-language newspaper *Afinskiy Kur'er* (Athens Courier) discussed the pro-Russian approach of ANEL in general.

Several questions remain, however. Are pro-Russian sentiments indeed important for ANEL? Will ANEL contribute to the strengthening of SYRIZA's pro-Russian positions? Will the new coalition government push for lifting the EU sanctions against Russia that is escalating its invasion of Ukraine?

Doubtlessly, Russia will try to capitalize both on the victory of SYRIZA and the formation of the SYRIZA/ANEL coalition government. Putin has already congratulated Tsipras on his party's victory saying that he is *"confident that Russia and Greece will continue to develop their traditionally constructive cooperation in all areas and will work together effectively to resolve current European and global problems".* Russian ambassador Andrey Maslov entered SYRIZA main office just after SYRIZA's electoral victory.

Kammenos' visit to Moscow was most likely connected to the possibility of the formation of the SYRIZA/ANEL coalition government. At the same time, Avramidis visited the General Consulate of Russia in Thessaloniki on 23 January 2015, i.e. just a few days before the parliamentary elections, to discuss, with Consul General Aleksey Popov, the renewal of the cooperation between Greece and Russia, as well as lifting the sanctions against Russia.

SYRIZA and Hamas

The party has constantly identified itself with the Palestinian cause and its program includes a demand for abolition of Greece's military cooperation with Israel and the support for the creation of a Palestinian state within the 1967 borders. Israel and Greece have enjoyed a strong relationship and cooperation since 2008 in several aspects of military, intelligence, economy and culture.

Alexis Tsipras' party colleagues and his own inner circle have repeatedly attacked Israel and the "Zionists" claiming that they are not anti-Semitic, just "anti-Zionist." Syriza's former head, Nikos Konstandopoulos, has consistently offered his services as a defense lawyer for convicted and alleged Arab terrorists who have been arrested in Greece.

Last year, Tsipras stated that "the world should make every possible effort so that Israel ends its criminal attack and brutality against Palestinians."

"Seeing Israel killing children in Palestine is unacceptable. We should unite our voices and forces so as to live in peace, expressing our solidarity to the Palestinian people," he said during a march in Athens against Israel's Operation Protective Edge against Hamas in Gaza last summer.

"When civilians and children are killed at beaches facing the same sea that borders on the European continent, we cannot remain passive, because if this happens on the other side of the Mediterranean today, it can happen on our own side tomorrow," he said. Alexis Tsipras, the new prime minister, was hailed by Hamas for his opposition to "Israeli crimes, aggression, and siege on Gaza," according to the Ma'an news agency.

The victory of the Greek Syriza Party, which won 149 out of 300 parliamentary seats, has brought major concerns for Israel but was welcomed by the Palestinians. The radical left-wing party scored a decisive victory in the snap elections held Jan. 25 in Greece.

Palestinian President Mahmoud Abbas as well as the left-wing Popular Front for the Liberation of Palestine and the Islamic Hamas movement were among those to congratulate the Greek people with the election results.

In 2011, party leader Alexis Tsipras, 40, was among the Greek activists who were scheduled to board a Gaza-bound flotilla called The Audacity of Hope, aimed at breaking Gaza's siege. The flotilla never left the Greek port having been stopped by the Greek government, most likely under pressure from Israel.

Tsipras was also a vocal opponent to the Israeli war on Gaza last summer during an anti-Israel demonstration in Athens at the time. "Seeing Israel killing children in Palestine is unacceptable. We should unite our voices and forces so as to live in peace, expressing our solidarity to the Palestinian people," he said.

It is not clear how quickly the newly elected prime minister will move in fulfilling his party's promise to recognize the state of Palestine. In Western Europe, only Sweden has publicly recognized Palestinian statehood.

Tsipras' success sent shock waves to Israel. Leading newspapers lamented the bad news that this success will have for Israeli-Greek relations. Israeli media reported that since 2008 Israel has enjoyed very close ties with Greece. Some Israeli analysts, however, argue that when in power, candidates often tone down their rhetoric.

The victory of the Syriza Party has given hope to many Palestinians that global popular changes are being translated to more serious political empowerment. While it is unclear if the Greek victory will result in a speedy recognition of Palestinian statehood in the way the results of the Swedish elections did, the news from Athens can only be described as badly needed good news for the Palestinians.

Nationalist partners

Socialist party Syriza might have won a surprising victory in Greece's elections but it will only be able to govern with the help of the Independent Greeks.

The party was founded in early 2012 by leader Panos Kammenos, Greece's former shipping minister who defected from the centre-right New Democracy party along with several fellow MPs.

Its founding declaration vowed to end the "national humiliation and violent economic attack" on Greece in measures imposed by the European Commission, European Central Bank, and International Monetary Fund.

The party immediately took a socially right-wing stance, supporting patriotism and the role of the Greek Orthodox Church in family life and education.

The Independent Greeks vocally oppose immigration and multiculturalism, emphasizing the importance of "Greek history and culture".

Ankara is curious to find out whether Panos Kammenos, the new defense minister of Greece, will continue with his campaign rhetoric or act like a proper statesman. A senior security official in Ankara said: "If he continues with his populist pre-election language in his new post, this will be a worrying development for us. But we have to see how he performs first."

In foreign policy affairs, Kammenos is an unadulterated nationalist. Rejecting EU and IMF policies on Greece, he accused the EU of using Greece as a guinea pig. He accused Greek politicians of turning Greece into a "concubine of Europe," and started wearing a T-shirt with the inscription "Greece is not for sale" following the increased pace of privatization.

Kammenos, a devout Orthodox, homophobic and fervently against illegal immigrants, was also branded as anti-Semitic because of his recent remarks. Kammenos is a dedicated anti-Turkey politician. He had actually protested against Prime Minister Ahmet Davutoglu during his Athens visit in December. He was even declared as "undesirable" by Turkey because of his unpleasant references to Turk-Muslim minorities in Greece, one newspaper reported.

The most serious concern in Turkey after Kammenos became defense minister was whether the minor frictions two countries experience at times at the Aegean Sea and in Aegean airspace could escalate to major incidents.

Although Turkey and Greece had been rivals in NATO for many years, the NATO umbrella enabled them to work together and avoid clashes. Today, Syriza's anti-NATO stance and the anti-Turkey position of Kammenos have become a true riddle both for NATO and Turkey.

In his first remarks after taking over his portfolio, Kammenos said military salaries will be increased, new funds will be found to develop the military, new investments will be channeled to the defense industry and Greece's security policy will be expanded with new pacts outside of NATO.

Pro-Russia and China views of the new government and its declared need for another alliance to balance NATO could well provide China and Russia with the entry they need to increase their effectiveness in the Aegean Sea and eastern Mediterranean.

To predict how these developments will affect the Middle East, one has to look at the map. Greece's geographical position allows it considerable leeway in controlling the Aegean Sea, which is the Black Sea's access to warm seas and to the eastern Mediterranean, which is increasingly important because of the civil war in Syria and prospects for natural energy resourcesin the region.

Greece's role in controlling access to the eastern Mediterranean can be amplified if it can develop warm relations with Egypt, which means many will be watching what relations the new Greek government will develop with the regime of President Abdel Fattah al-Sisi in Cairo. If Greece and Egypt can agree on closer ties with Russia, one could easily forecast difficult days for NATO, the United States and Turkey in the eastern Mediterranean.

Then there is Israel. Will Israel handle its relations with Greece by reacting to the anti-Semitic narrative of Kammenos or as dictated by its strategic interests in the region? Whether Israel opts for close or cool relations with the Greek government is a critical dynamic for the balance of security in the eastern Mediterranean.

In short, political preferences of the new Greek government and its new defense minister Kammenos could be the harbingers of important developments for Turkey and the region. The question that needs answers most for Washington, European capitals, Moscow, Beijing and Ankara is whether the Greek government adheres to its pre-election discourse and adopts a revisionist security policy or stays with its traditional alignment with Europe and NATO.

If Kammenos sticks to his populist discourse, the Greek navy and air force will be very busy and tired. What is more worrying is that it will also mean much more fatigue for the Turkish navy and air force.

ISBN 9781512311686

9 781512 311686

Brad Power

MOSSAD

SAUDI ARABIA -- MOSSAD

HAND IN HAND

AGAINST

IRAN

- How Riyad's rulers receive intelligence from Mossad
- Why ISIS doesn't attack Israel
- Why Neocons love Bandar Bin Sultan

Exclusive Revelations by *Best Seller* Writer Brad Power